THINKING
FOR A CHANGE

Transforming your life by transforming your thoughts

Alice Maryniuk

THIS BOOK IS AN EXCELLENT GUIDE FOR LIVING A HAPPY, FULFILLED AND SUCCESSFUL LIFE.

Bob Burg, Coauthor of *The Go-Giver*

ISBN 10: 1-933817-47-X
ISBN 13: 978-1933817-47-7

Book Cover designed by Vivek Shenoy
Email: vivekdshenoy@gmail.com
Canada phone: 1-604-825-3058

Editorial assistance was provided by Michael Kerry

Published by: Profits Publishing
http://profitspublishing.com

Canadian Address

1265 Charter Hill Drive
Coquitlam, BC, V3E 1P1
Phone: 604-941-3041
Fax: 604-944-7993

US Address

1300 Boblett Street
Unit A-218
Blaine, WA 98230
Phone: 866-492-6623
Fax: 250-493-6603

Library of Congress Cataloging-in-Publication Data

Maryniuk, Alice.
    Thinking for a change / Alice Maryniuk.

This Book is dedicated to my husband Bob and our two beautiful children Josiah and Evangeline. I will always be grateful for all you have taught me and for your love and support over the years. A special thanks to my two sisters Jo and Beth for believing in my dreams and supporting me in my endeavors. Thank you to my mom who has faithfully prayed for me my entire life. A special thanks to all my mentors and coaches who have patiently assisted me in my weaknesses and shortcomings. My life has been enriched by all of you who never gave up on me.

Maria
God is working in you!
Might&lly

Also McApple

THINKING FOR A CHANGE *by Alice Maryniuk*

Learn how to transform your life by transforming your thoughts.

TABLE OF CONTENTS   **PAGE**

i

SHAR**E**
Chapter 5
Transform Your Economical Situation To Gain Financial Freedom

Thinking for a Change

WHAT OTHERS SAY ABOUT THIS BOOK

Alice's book has demonstrated great insight for me on how I can change my beliefs and easily change my life for the better. Her book is filled with examples, techniques, insights, and questions that all make for useful tools. It has helped me to clarify some priorities and confront issues head on. Great book!

Bob Burnham

Author of the # 1 Amazon Best Selling Book *101 Reasons Why You Must Write A Book - How to Make A Six Figure Income by Writing and Publishing Your Own Book*

Don't be fooled by the compact size of this book. This is a terrific collection of power tools, tools that can change your life for the better if you use them. This is my favourite kind of book: philosophical and practical at the same time. If you want a richer, happier life, this is a great place to begin.

Barbara J Winter

Author, Making a Living Without a Job

This book is filled with lots of good, practical, proactive advice that can be applied to anyone's life. Alice writes with feeling, compassion, and common sense. There are few books that blend the practical with the scriptural without becoming preachy and overly new age centered. This book is a must read for anyone who needs guidance, both for the client and the counselor.

Suzanne Blakley-Oaks

Program Coordinator/ Business Advisor

Fraser Valley Self Employment Program

When I met Alice about twenty years ago, she was not so confident, not so organized, and did not believe in herself. Many tests and trials of life have made Alice who she is today. Her life experiences of triumph pave a path for others to encounter positive change in their lives. This book is full of relevant and practical insights that are invigorating and enlightening.

Elfrieda Toews

Mentor and Friend

This book will help you evaluate your life's goals, target problem areas, and develop consistency to complete existing goals. This book is designed to inspire you to get moving. It is practical in nature and designed to inspire you so you naturally inspire others. Alice Maryniuk has written *Thinking For A Change* keeping in mind the needs of individuals from all walks of life. You will want to refer to it time after time.

Ida Leguizamon

Missionary to Argentina

This is an excellent book to formulate constructive changes in life. It influenced me to take further steps to think for a change and be all that God made me to be. I am using this book as a blueprint to make adjustments in different areas of my life. Alice's expertise and insight into these areas prepared a way for my personal growth and spiritual development.

Colleen J. Gerwing

Business Owner/Transportation Consultant

Power Painting & Interior Finishes

Alice Maryniuk has written a winner! It is scriptural. It is easy to read. It is life changing. In her own unique way, Alice has shared the odyssey of her own life in a vulnerability that is believable and easy to follow. The steps she has provided are easy to follow and will aid any person who chooses to avail themselves in their life growth. There is no doubt in my mind that you have in your hand a tool for positive life change. I plan on using it as a tool in my own ministry.

Pastor Carson Jamieson

Elder/Teacher - Abbotsford Christian Assembly

Teaching the Nations

Alice's book contains powerful principles that can change your thinking and your life. It is said it takes twenty-eight days to establish new habits. Anyone who commits to doing the exercises will greatly benefit and see transformation take place in their life. I highly recommend it.

Patricia McQuarrie

Speaker, Prayer Minister

This book is a practical tool for anyone who is serious about making constructive changes in their lives. Each chapter offers powerful tools to examine and question your life and your way of thinking. Regardless of a person's religious beliefs, this book applies to all walks of life. I recommend this book to everyone who is on the road to success.

Shakiba Ahani

Founder of A New You Coaching

This book is an excellent guide for living a happy, fulfilled and successful life.

Bob Burg

Coauthor of *The Go-Giver*

Thinking for a Change

INTRODUCTION

For my entire life I have been fascinated with Cinderella stories. An example is the movie *Les Misérables* where Jean Valjean, a heartless convict, is transformed into becoming a mayor by a priest's act of mercy. And in the movie *Sabrina*, the chauffeur's daughter moves to Paris and changes from a dull-looking wallflower into a confident and assertive "dazzling" young lady.

I am captivated by such stories; I am encouraged and inspired to change like that myself. I've come to realize that, unlike Hollywood fantasies where the handsome prince finds Cinderella and suddenly everything changes, we each can become an agent of positive change.

Real change is the result of thinking about the differences between where you are and where you want and desire to be. To experience change you have to visualize change. This requires thinking for a change.

You must engage your mind by reflecting on the direction you want your life to take. You should use your mind for the purpose of stewardship and management towards your personal success.

Do you believe that you are a victim of circumstances and other people's opinion of you? Do you realize that by taking control of your thoughts you can take control of your life? You are responsible for your life. You are where you are in life because of your thoughts and the choices you have made.

If you have the habit of thinking negatively then you will produce negative results. You cannot stop thoughts from popping into your head, but you can replace negative thinking with positive thinking. Thinking negatively is a habit established over time. You can change your life powerfully by starting the habit of thinking empowering thoughts that support your dreams.

This book is designed to be a guide for managing your life and managing your mind. It will cause you to seriously consider the five key areas of your life: your self, your relationships, your accomplishments, your health, and your finances.

Changing your thoughts requires a desire and a commitment to implement new ideas. You must reserve a time for creative thinking and be intentional about how you think. Pay attention to what you believe. Get into the habit of writing down ideas, evaluating them, and implementing the good ones. When you upgrade your mind you will upgrade your life. Turn your thoughts into allies and your mind into a weapon to wage war on lifelessness.

As you read this book I encourage you to draw your own conclusions. Interpret the information to create and implement new ideas into your life. Be honest with yourself and be willing to confront areas in your life. The truth that comes from understanding yourself can destroy denial and self-neglect.

Letting go of old thinking patterns is necessary to embrace new ways of thinking. Letting go can be difficult because it's like a death in the family. It's about parting with a life, saying "good-bye" to old thinking patterns and old ways of doing things. Changing your thoughts involves acknowledging your fears and disappointments—and that takes courage and commitment. Embracing change is the essence of life. In order to take necessary steps to dig yourself out of the rubble you find yourself in, you must start thinking for a change.

Change always starts with you and it starts with how you think. Thinking makes the difference in how you interpret and respond to your life's events. If you think the world is against you and that no one loves you, that is how you will experience life. You will act in a way that rejects love and acceptance even if you already have it in great abundance.

On the other hand, you will be received according to the value you place on yourself. If you act like a leader you will be perceived as one. If you act as though you are successful you will be perceived as successful. If you know that you are loved and accepted you will act with love and acceptance, drawing even more of the same into your life. Your thinking is like a magnet and others will be attracted to it.

As for me, I had to get out of the tedious rat race and slow down my pace of living. Negative patterns of thinking were so deeply formed that I was just living my life on auto-pilot. Then I had "crashed and burned" and the reality of where my thoughts had taken me was a sobering message. Now it was time to be conscious of my thoughts and monitor my belief system.

The process was not a quick one. The first step for me was to take care of the worn-out part of me. I had to stop working insane hours. I went for long walks, slept, journaled, read, cried, enrolled in classes, and received personal counseling.

The caterpillar will stay a caterpillar unless it goes into the cocoon stage. The cocoon is the place of letting go of old thoughts that have kept you captive. Dynamic change wants you to emerge as a beautiful butterfly; yet it's not without a fight. When the butterfly emerges you will realize that the fight was well worth the reward.

I've heard it said that the only ones who like a change are babies. Yet embracing and welcoming positive change into our lives is a sign of healthy maturity. Even difficult experiences can create a way for positive change if we allow it.

We have a choice to be a victim or a victor. Victims blame others for their lifestyle and waste time thinking of new excuses. But if you are to succeed, there must come a time when you take responsibility for your own life. Change is a natural part of life and it doesn't need to be feared. Taking a proactive role in your life will allow you to embrace change in positive ways.

This book provides you with essential principles to adapt into your life in the five key areas of life. Self-esteem, Health, Accomplishments, Relationships and Economics are the five key areas. So just remember the acronym SHARE. This book will help you to make a significant difference in your life by "thinking for a change."

You attract what you think you deserve. Your reality is simply a reflection of your thoughts. The more you are willing to allow yourself to have, the more you will have. Focus on moving forward. Look where you want to go. Ask for what you want. Focus on the positive. Enjoy the process so much that the result doesn't matter. Do the things you do for the pure pleasure of doing them. Relax and allow things to come to you. Make a difference in your world by thinking for a change.

After you read this book, I would love to hear from you. I want to hear your success stories because that is what this book is all about. Do keep in touch.

For your free 35 Simple Secrets Towards A Life Makeover (value $19), visit our website at www.dynamicchanges.ca.

Thinking for a Change

CHAPTER 1
TRANSFORM YOURSELF TO CREATE A FULFILLING LIFE

Changing your life starts with changing your thoughts. Our thoughts could be called self-talk and we talk to ourselves all the time. The way we establish a relationship with ourselves is determined by the way we talk to ourselves. Sometimes we talk quite roughly and harshly to ourselves, with words that we would never dream of using if we were talking to a friend.

CHANGING YOUR BELIEFS CHANGES YOUR BEHAVIOUR

Turning negative self-talk into positive affirmations is essential for positive change. The statements that we make to ourselves have a powerful effect upon our behaviour and actions. An

1

affirmation can be what we know to be true in our head, but don't yet believe in our heart. For example, we might know that to err is human, but do we give ourselves permission to make mistakes?

If we want to change our actions and behaviour we must change our beliefs. For example, I might be telling myself to stop being so shy when I enter a room full of strangers. But the reason I say nothing, turn red in the face and become nervous is because I believe that I am ugly and stupid. My behaviour, feelings, and emotions are a result of my belief. As I become aware of my negative beliefs and start replacing them with positive ones, I will see a change in my behaviour.

DEAL WITH FEELINGS APPROPRIATELY

Feelings should not be ignored nor should they control you. If you feel angry, your feelings are telling you that something is wrong and change is needed. Acknowledge why you feel angry, identify the cause, and work towards a solution.

If you feel you hate yourself you should start changing what can be changed and accept what can't be changed. Stop complaining and stop putting yourself down. Speaking curses over yourself is hindering and limiting you from living up to your potential. Be aware of your weaknesses, but do not be discouraged by them. Recognize your strong traits and take the time necessary to develop them. Patting yourself on the back for an achievement rather than having to depend on others for approval is a liberating act.

TAKE CARE TO NURTURE YOURSELF

Don't be afraid about what others think. What's important is that you love and accept yourself. When you love and accept yourself, you are not looking for the approval of others. When you accept yourself you are giving yourself freedom to be loved. Engaging in self-care and nurturing yourself develops self-respect. A few years ago I asked myself three questions:

1. Have I learned how to be a friend to myself?
2. Have I discovered how to nurture myself with self-care?
3. Am I really happy with myself?

As I responded with a resounding "No," tears welled up inside, too powerful to hold back any longer. I had been starving for self-acceptance. I needed to give myself permission to stumble as well as to sprout wings.

For years I had a wild woman inside insulting my every move. The bully that lived in my brain was the cause of my self-hate. Self-criticism kept me small and self-absorbed. Learning to live a life of self-honour and self-respect did not come easy for me. I had to learn to be kind to myself. It is love, not anger, that inspires right thinking. We cannot fool ourselves in thinking that we are capable of loving others when we are full of self-hate. Contentment in life starts with liking yourself. If you don't take care of yourself, you will always be at the mercy of others, and highly vulnerable to their opinions, rejection, and criticism.

BECOME AUTHENTIC

As we begin to change what we believe about ourselves, it is essential that we become authentic. Being authentic involves being the same person in private as we are in public. It involves being true to ourselves and aligning our lives with our values. Having every part flow together eliminates the feeling of being scattered. We become less awkward, gain assurance, and begin to see lasting results. Our thoughts are genuine, accurate, and true, and we are exactly as we appear or claim to be.

MAKE UP YOUR OWN MIND

Identify and write down anything that is making you feel unworthy, ashamed, or inferior. Ask yourself if you believe that others are better or more qualified than you are. This could be related to work, school, finances, sociability, or appearance. Remember that no one is perfect. Even the most confident people have insecurities. In any aspect of our lives, we may feel uncertain until we gain competence.

During my childhood, I would act the way other people thought I should. Being the youngest of six children made it difficult for me to make my own decisions and choose for myself. It took me many years to discover what I really enjoyed or what I liked. Even as an adult I struggled to make choices that truly suited me. I had to learn how to weed out every thought that was not acceptable to me. I had to accept and keep only those thoughts that lined up with the way I wanted to be.

I began to examine and challenge my thoughts. I wrote down negative beliefs and started replacing them with positive ones. I have included some examples of negative beliefs and I invite you to take note of the ones you believe and add more of your own.

- I believe that I do not deserve anything better
- I magnify every setback as proof of failure
- I create a self-fulfilling prophecy of unworthiness
- I tell myself that not trying is better than looking bad
- I believe that others are more valuable than I am

- I expect others to approve of me when I do not accept myself
- I believe I am a victim of my circumstances
- _____
- _____

DISCOVER YOUR STRENGTHS AND YOUR TALENTS

Make a list of all the positive qualities that you have and focus on your strengths. Take some personality assessments. I have found CRG and Myers-Briggs really helpful for myself and for my clients. There's also a really good book called _Please Understand Me_ by Kiersey.

Do not be afraid to project your strengths and qualities to others. By doing so, you reinforce those ideas in your mind and encourage your growth in a positive direction. Identify your talents. Talents are natural abilities and desires that you were born with. Most people take their talents for granted because they are so used to being naturally good at them. They assume that a talent (for example neat handwriting) comes as easily for others as it does for them. This is not the case. It takes self-observation to discover your talents, and then you can develop them. It could be artistic, technical, mental, or physical.

HERE ARE SOME QUESTIONS TO ASK YOURSELF

1. What do I love to do and need to be dragged away from doing?

   _____

   _____

   _____

   _____

   _____

2. What do I enjoy doing and seem to be naturally good at?

   _____

   _____

   _____

   _____

3. What work seems like play to me?

   _____

   _____

   _____

   _____

4. What am I enthusiastic about?

   _____

   _____

   _____

   _____

5. What are some things I would like to explore and find out if I enjoy doing them?

_____

_____

_____

_____

6. What do I like to read about, write about, or talk about?

_____

_____

_____

_____

7. What do others compliment me about?

_____

_____

_____

_____

CHANGE YOUR BELIEFS

Focus on the good things in your life even when dealing with problems. Learn to be thankful for what you do have. By acknowledging and appreciating what you do have, you can combat the feeling of being incomplete and unsatisfied. Avoid feeling sorry for yourself. Engaging in self-pity is a waste of time.

Here are some examples of a new set of beliefs. As you read them make a note of the ones that you want to adapt. Write them on 3" by 5" cards and repeat these affirmations throughout the day.

- All humans have value including myself
- I learn from my mistakes and become a better person because of it
- I am beautiful, intelligent and worthy of respect

- I am loved and accepted
- I am significant, worthwhile, and uniquely made
- I easily forgive myself
- I develop my creative talents
- I am willing to try new things
- I can say "no" when necessary
- I am fun to be with
- I receive feedback and it helps me to grow
- I am a quick learner and enjoy learning new skills
- _____
- _____
- _____

QUESTIONS TO THINK ABOUT

1. What negative thoughts do I believe about myself (either past or present)?

_____

_____

_____

_____

_____

2. How can I turn those thoughts into positive affirmations?

_____

_____

_____

_____

_____

3. How can I demonstrate self-care?

_____

_____

_____

_____

_____

4. What qualities do I appreciate about myself?

_____

_____

_____

_____

_____

5. What are some things I want to change about myself?

_____

_____

_____

_____

Thinking for a Change

CHAPTER 2

TRANSFORM YOUR PHYSICAL HEALTH TO ACHIEVE STRENGTH AND ENERGY

You are your best and most valuable asset. Therefore you must take care of yourself. One of the workshops I do is called "Take Care," and in it I refer to the goose that lays the golden eggs. If you want any golden eggs, you have to take care of the goose. Start noticing what gives you energy and what depletes your energy. You only get one body, so taking care of it is vital.

LEARN TO FEEL COMFORTABLE IN YOUR OWN SKIN

Get rid of any pesky imperfection that is bothering you about your body (such as bad teeth, unattractive hair style, unwanted hair, or a mole).

Get into shape and maybe even hire a professional trainer.

As a child growing up, I believed I was ugly. Ugly was one of my names that I would answer to and each time I would see my reflection in the mirror, I would confirm to myself that I was indeed ugly. I was out of shape; had fine, greasy hair; had red, blotchy skin; had strong body odour; had short, stubby fingernails; had yellow teeth; had bad breath; had poor posture; and wore drab-looking clothes.

In grade ten my sister introduced me to the daughter of one of her friends. The daughter was the same age as me and to this day is still a good friend of mine. This friend, Debbie, was a model and she and her friend Julia helped me to change the way I felt about myself. They helped me to get a hair style that suited my face shape, coloured my hair blond, and showed me how to apply makeup. They took me shopping and helped me to create a dressy-casual wardrobe of colours and styles that suited my body type. Dressing the part has helped me to get rid of the belief that I was ugly.

I began to implement exercise as part of my lifestyle. I walked or rode my bicycle everywhere. Very seldom would I drive. Twice I ran in the Vancouver Sun Run and ran ten kilometers in fifty-nine minutes. I worked out at the gym and invested in a personal trainer. I cut out the sweets, fried foods, white sugar, and white flour. I took daily supplements, drank lots of water, and ate fresh fruits and vegetables daily.

It is said that you can't judge a book by its cover. Yet reality proved to me that people would treat me differently based on the way I looked. We can all come up with excuses when we don't want to do something. A common excuse is, "But it costs too much to stay healthy and look good." My comment to that is that you either pay now or you pay later; either way you pay. You have a choice to take care of your body now, or pay later in hospital bills, surgery, and medication. Maintaining good health is an investment that you will appreciate in your older years.

DEAL WITH STRESS APPROPRIATELY

Take a weekly Sabbath, a day of rest. Let it be a day to do whatever you want. Take a nap, take a bath, read in a park, sit on the beach, take a weekend retreat, or watch the sunset.

The number one cause of health problems is a weak immune system and this is affected by stress. A lot of stress in not necessarily caused by what happens to us, but by our interpretation of what happens. Self-talk has an incredible effect on us and we need to take inventory on what we are saying.

Here are some examples of beliefs that cause excess stress:

- I'm so stressed out
- You make me so angry
- I hate this job
- I have to do everything around here

If this applies to you, it's time to change your belief system. One way that I have transformed the way I think is by speaking positive affirmations over myself and doing so has helped me deal with stress in a constructive way. It's changing the way I think. I used to be afraid of bad things happening to me and fearful that I would make wrong choices. This all changed as I started to speak forth positive things into my life. Here is an example of one of my positive statements."

- "Every element of my day lines up with my great purpose and the destiny of my life. I break evil and inappropriate thought patterns in my mind. I cancel the effect of negative, self-defeating thought processes. I declare a prophetic upgrading of my thought-life which grants me new ways of thinking, new ways of working, and new ways of living. I receive the supernatural discipline to implement them. My emotions are sound and stable. I am healthy and physically fit. I live in perfect health and healing. My body operates in excellence. Every cell, valve, tissue, and organ of my body functions in perfection."

Saying this has helped to build confidence in me that with God's help I can conquer whatever comes my way. It's helped to create a positive mindset that replaced the old "victim" mentality.

UNDERSTAND THAT YOUR RESPONSE AFFECTS YOUR OUTCOME

I encourage you to become aware of what you believe concerning your body and your physical health. Write down your beliefs in your journal and begin to change negative thoughts into positive ones. In my classes on dealing with stress I share the formula for success. It is $E + R = O$. Events plus Response equals Outcome. Two people can experience the same event, but based on what they believe about it, the outcome for one person will be different from the outcome for the other.

A few years ago, when I was teaching in Surrey, I met a person who had to commute every day from Abbotsford to Surrey, just as I did. I said to her "Isn't it a pain driving in all that rush hour traffic every day?" She replied with, "Oh I love the drive every day and it gives me a chance to unwind and leave my problems at home or work." I thought or

she was joking, but I soon realized she was serious. We were both experiencing rush hour traffic, but my outcome was a lot worse than hers. It was a lesson for me to change the way I viewed the event.

What things have you been telling yourself that have been causing excess stress in your life? This does affect your physical health. Begin today by replacing those negative thoughts with good things.

In 1993 a traumatic accident threw me into a depression and chronic pain for five years. I was diagnosed with chronic Fibromyalgia, Ankylosing Spondylitis (a type of arthritis), and chronic depression. The doctors told me that I would have to be on antidepressants the rest of my life and that I would never run again. I had to choose how I would respond to that event. I could decide to give in and become a victim or I could do my best to overcome these obstacles.

It was a struggle indeed, but with God's help and the help of supportive friends, my health is better today then it's ever been. Yet as tragic as that experience was, it was a catalyst for bringing me to the point of some radical changes in my life. I started attending anger management classes to deal with anger that had been stored inside and was now surging out of me like a volcano. I began to receive counseling to change my habits of passiveness into skills with assertiveness. This in return helped me to get my health back on track. In 1997 I became a Life Coach and over the years I have helped hundreds of people overcome obstacles that I once encountered.

ESTABLISH NEW EATING HABITS

Here are some basic tips on developing new eating habits that proved helpful to me. As you read them, ask yourself which ones you could put into action for your lifestyle.

1. Eat slowly and chew food thoroughly. Stop eating at the first signs of fullness.
2. Do not eat after 6 pm. Your body does not have a chance to use up those calories and excess food sits in your stomach while you sleep.
3. Select foods by nutritional value. The purpose of eating is to meet your body's physical need of nourishment, not your emotional needs.
4. Avoid salt, sugar, caffeine, white flour, canned goods, and processed foods. These foods contain a lot of calories, but not an adequate amount of nutrients.
5. Drink eight cups of water a day. Most bodies are dehydrated. Water occupies 92 percent of

our blood plasma, 80 percent of our muscle mass, and 60 percent of our red blood cells.

6. Avoid fried foods and, if possible, use waterless cookware. Do not over-cook your food. This will help conserve vitamins, especially vitamins A and C, because you cook at a lower heat.

7. Do not have junk food in the house. This makes it easier to not eat it and it helps to make this a family effort. When we are craving something, it is usually an indication that we lack nutrition.

8. Eat fresh fruits, vegetables, nuts, and grains. I also eat fish and chicken. I don't eat a lot of pasta, but when I do, I use whole wheat, not white flour. Eating the right kinds of food will help keep your energy level high and maintain your concentration and ability to handle stress.

9. Take supplements. Because most of our produce is picked green it is impossible to receive all the nutrients once found in fruits and vegetables. Therefore it is necessary to take supplements that are natural plant source and none that are synthetic.

ADAPT A LIFESTYLE OF PHYSICAL ACTIVITY

When it comes to exercise I would recommend hiring a fitness trainer. You can join a gym and sometimes it includes the price of a personal trainer. The gym I attend does not include the price of a trainer, so I pay for my personal trainer. When looking for the right trainer, understand your fitness goals. Trainers specialize in certain areas such as losing weight, recovering from injuries, increasing your endurance, being fit, and gaining strength and muscles.

When I first hired my trainer, my goal for exercise was to get rid of pain. The lightest move would cause a cramp; I had constant pain in my neck and shoulders from stress and pain in my back from weak abdominal muscles and poor posture.

I made appointments with my trainer every six to eight weeks. He showed me a new workout every time and I was disciplined enough to do it regularly. For some of my clients, this is not the case. They meet with their trainer at the gym three times a week and that motivates them to exercise. Others don't like going to the gym, so the trainer comes to their home. Some like attending group classes and that works well for them. There are also really good fitness magazines available with motivating pictures and helpful tools. One client plans her own routine using the workouts from "Oxygen Women's Fitness" magazine. As with most new activities, you must experiment and find out what works best for you.

Here are some guidelines for beginning an exercise program. In the beginning do not overdo it. Be aware of signals from your body because they will tell you if you are being too hard on yourself.

1. Take a thirty-minute walk four or five times a week.

2. Find a cardiovascular activity that you enjoy. This could include biking, running, tennis, hiking, swimming, dancing, or whatever sport appeals to you.

3. Add variety to your exercise routine to help keep it fun and exciting.

4. Start with a five-minute warm-up. This should include stretching, bending, and rolling your joints.

5. Cardiovascular activities are to get your heart rate up and burn calories. Start with ten or twenty minutes and work up to forty minutes or so.

6. Start off with lower weights and more repetitions—two or three sets of fifteen reps. Breathe deeply through your nose and exhale out your mouth. Inhale on the easy part and exhale on the harder part. Go at a slow, conscious pace, keeping proper body posture.

7. Cool down. Keep moving, walking slowly for five minutes or so. Hold each stretch for thirty seconds. This helps to lessen muscle soreness the next day.

RECALL THE REWARDS OF EXERCISING

Here's how you'll benefit from exercise:

- It opens your sweat glands and keeps your complexion clear and healthy.
- It strengthens your muscles and makes you stronger.
- It helps blood and oxygen circulation.

- It gives you a good feeling about yourself and a sense of accomplishment.
- It firms and tones your body.
- It helps to release tension and anxiety, and it gives you a sound sleep.

LEARN TO LAUGH

One key element in increasing your health is learning not to take yourself too seriously. Learning to laugh with yourself and others is a gift we can all develop. Proverbs 15:15 says that he who is of a merry heart has a continual feast, regardless of circumstances. Proverbs 17:22 says that a merry heart does well like a medicine.

One of my first jobs after graduating from high school was being a cashier at a drug store. It was on November 1st and I was eagerly assisting customers, when suddenly the doors flew open and there stood two men, with women's nylons covering their heads and each of them was carrying a gun pointing directly at me.

I immediately thought that they got their days mixed up because yesterday was Halloween. Nevertheless it was a great costume and it looked so real. I was ready to congratulate them when suddenly one of them stuck his gun in my face and told me to put all the money in a bag. Putting the money in a bag was a major decision.

We had several bags to choose from and I wondered which bag should I use? A small bag might break because money can be heavy but a big bag might be too bulky. I couldn't make up my mind, so I asked him which bag he wanted. He pointed his gun at my nose and told me that I needed to hurry up.

I started bagging the money, but when I came to the pennies, I didn't know if he wanted them. I asked him, "Do you want pennies? They are heavy and not worth much, but if you want them you can have them?" With his gun pointed at my forehead, he said, "I am going to blow your head off." In my shock, I wondered what my head would look like flying through the air.

His buddy came running towards me from the pharmacy and was holding a bag full of money, pills, and medication. My bag was neatly rolled up with scotch tape securely holding everything in place. Ripping the bag out of my hand, he gave me strict instructions to stay where I was. They ran off into the dark night, leaving me with a sensation of confusion.

After a few minutes a woman came into the store with a description of the men and the vehicle. Very soon the police arrived and I was told they caught the guys. The men were high on drugs and the guns were loaded.

During this time, my sister Beth was waiting for me in the car. By the time I got into the car I was crying uncontrollably. She asked me what happened and as I told her the story she burst into laughter. I thought, how can she be so inconsiderate and laugh when I almost got killed?

She apologized to me, still laughing, and said she couldn't help it. She said that it just sounded so funny, "What kind of bag do you want? Would you like pennies with that?" I had to admit that she was right and we both enjoyed a good laugh.

Maybe this story of my lack of common sense can be a reminder to all of us to not take ourselves so seriously.

QUESTIONS TO THINK ABOUT

1. What new thoughts and affirmations do I want to establish regarding my physical body?

   _____

   _____

   _____

   _____

2. What new habits can I adapt into my lifestyle to enhance my physical body and my appearance?

_____

_____

_____

_____

CHAPTER 3
TRASFORM YOUR ACCOMPLISHMENTS TO MASTER YOUR DESTINY

Celebrate your success. Take stock of what you have already accomplished and write it down. Take time to bask in the love you feel. Appreciate what you do have. I enjoy scrapbooking and every month I collect pictures of all the things I have accomplished monthly. Several times I look at it and it reminds me of all the goals I have completed and it motivates me to continue on.

UNCLUTTER YOUR ENVIRONMENT

Achieving great things involves having a clear mind. In 1993 a car hit me on my bicycle and I landed head-first on the pavement. Aside from other complications, I had a minor concussion and short term memory lost. It took me years to recover from it. It was a long journey in learning how to have a sound mind. But one very important aspect that I discovered was how having an uncluttered environment affected my mind.

Having my house full of chaos affected my mind and hindered me from fully concentrating on my priorities. Frustration set in and my time was taken up looking for lost items. I ended up forgetting important tasks and I started living life recklessly. I began to feel like a city under siege. The confusion of my environment began to create confusion in my mind.

I have discovered that having a clean and orderly environment brings peace to my mind. A clean home creates a peaceful and godly environment. For myself, because I can become easily distracted, having a clean home helps me to concentrate better. Playing relaxing music and having a clutter-free environment empowers and energizes me. Like a compass that leads me down the right path, setting my priorities straight helps bring clarity.

Is your environment in chaos? To change your ways that are out of control, you must change how you think and act about disorganization. Bad habits are like weeds and you must root them out. Why do you have a backlog of unpaid bills, emails to respond to, or phone calls to make? Are you overwhelmed by too much activity and not able to say "no" to over-commitment? Do you gain your sense of identity by wanting to do everything that is asked of you? Perhaps you don't feel worthy of being in control of your own choices. Start today by getting rid of everything you haven't used in the last year and stop living in the past. Clean up after yourself and don't leave messes everywhere. Set aside twenty minutes each evening to clean. Have a calendar where you plan and schedule your priorities. Set aside blocks of time for things that are important to you.

Creating and sustaining order will release you to be prepared, productive, and purposeful. Dealing with clutter in your home will assist you in bringing peace of mind. This includes self-observation, clarifying your roles in life, defining your job description, defining true success, developing your gifts, living in sync with your values, and reclaiming your finances.

DEAL WITH PROCRASTINATION

Achievements are accomplished by a series of small steps made over a long period of time. Accomplishments are fulfilled by conquering procrastination. Let's face it—we are all challenged with tasks that seem unpleasant, fearful, and mundane to us. Being disciplined to do what we know is right isn't always easy. Being a person of self-control involves overcoming procrastination. Procrastination is the habitual delay in starting a task or seeing it through to conclusion. It is making promises and breaking them. It is making excuses and blaming our circumstances. The longer we postpone what needs to be taken care of, the harder it gets to face the unpleasant task. Worry and guilt set in as we keep putting things off. Procrastination is a bad habit that can be changed, but it isn't always easy.

Here are some steps of action to take in helping you overcome procrastination:

1. Do not chastise yourself for past behaviour. Be confident that you can change this habit pattern.
2. On your next project or commitment, set realistic performance expectations for yourself. After doing so, check with another person whose opinion you respect. He or she

can confirm that your revised expectations are realistic.

3. Choose one project and break it into small, manageable parts. Smaller tasks are attractive because they are short, easy, and produce immediate gratification.

4. Put each small step onto your calendar.

5. Look for the positive. Create enthusiasm to counterbalance the unpleasantness.

6. Encourage yourself and remind yourself of all the benefits of accomplishing the task.

7. Start small. With taking one baby step at a time, you can defeat this habit. Aim to work twenty minutes on your task.

8. Barter the task with someone and do a task for them in exchange.

9. Do the most unpleasant thing early in the morning when you are fresh.

10. Remove distractions from the environment. Close the door, use an empty office, or go into another room.

11. Mix up the types of activities the project calls for: planning, talking, researching, and writing, for example.

12. Take regular breaks.

13. Reward yourself for good behaviour. Reading for pleasure, relaxing, participating in sports, visiting friends, travelling, going to dinner, and exercising can all be used as rewards.

Overcoming procrastination will help you feel better about yourself and you will gain confidence. You will be a person of integrity, living your lifestyle according to your values and priorities. You will be a person of your word, doing what you say. There are giants out there to overcome and as you conquer the giant of procrastination, you will have the confidence to defeat greater obstacles.

BECOME SKILLED AT MANAGING YOUR TIME

The way we spend and invest our time has a profound influence on our accomplishments. Time is one of our greatest assets. We all have twenty-four hours each day, but what we do with our time is the determining factor of our success or failure. Do we make the most of our time and utilize it to invest into our future? Or do we waste our time carelessly because we lack vision and purpose for our lives?

The average person's lifetime includes twenty years of sleeping, six years of watching television, five years of dressing and shaving, three years of waiting for others, one year on the telephone, and four months of tying shoes.

How you manage your time determines how you live your life. Without plans, you are easily sidetracked. The object is to plan the important activities every day and every week. Do you spend time with people you love and care about? Weed out people who truly waste your time, drag you down, or give you a pain. When times or circumstances change, revise your plans accordingly to fit the new conditions.

Take inventory of the activities you spend your time on. Look to areas that you can cut back on that someone else could do, or that really aren't important. Write down your goals to know what is most important to you. Try to do at least one thing each day towards accomplishing your goals. It could be making a phone call, sending an email, or researching information about some schooling you would like to take. Whatever it may be, spend your time on the things that mean the most for your life.

- Volunteer to do something only after you give up something else. Do not add more activities unless you subtract activities.
- When planning for the upcoming month, season, or year, schedule vacations, family time, and key social events first.

GET MUNDANE TASKS DONE QUICKLY

There is no question that there are mundane tasks that each of us must do. But there are ways to save and redeem your time. Here are some ways to do more in less time.

- Do errands together that are in the same location.
- Schedule time for routine tasks, such as laundry, that must be done to keep your life running smoothly.

- If you have a series of appointments in an office, schedule the next appointment before leaving the present one.
- Schedule multiple appointments for the same day.
- Buy greeting cards all at one time.
- When meeting with busy people, ask for the first appointment of the day. Your chances of having to wait are reduced.

LEARN TO DREAM AGAIN

Being a person of vision will aid you in being purposeful in the way you spend your time. When you understand your goals and have a clear vision of where you want to go, it will be easier to make right decisions that lead you closer to your dreams.

In Genesis 37:19 Joseph's brothers referred to Joseph as "the dreamer." Too often when we ask teenagers or adults, "What is your dream?" they don't know. They used to have dreams when they were little, but they've forgotten them. Some people are afraid to reveal what their dream is in case you try to steal it. It takes courage to take your dream out of the box, put it on like a coat, and start living it. I encourage you to reveal your dream and admit what you want.

Because I was the youngest of six I had many choices made for me from an early age, and that made it difficult for me to make my own choices. Even as an adult, it was difficult for me to order something off a menu. When I was shopping for clothes it was challenging for me to know which colours and styles I preferred. Getting to know yourself—your likes and dislikes, your strengths and weaknesses—is the beginning of the journey towards dreaming again.

I began to look through magazines to discover what types of clothes I liked. I started trying different types of food and I found out what I preferred. Designing collages and making scrapbooks of things I liked helped me to discover my goals, aspirations, and dreams. You too can start dreaming and becoming proactive in your life.

In the movie "The Ultimate Gift," one of Jason's tasks is to have a dream. He admits that he does not have one, but he can help others fulfill their dreams. If you don't have a dream of your own, you can start by helping others fulfill their dreams. Eventually you will begin to realize that there is something you want to accomplish.

Take some time to be alone and start writing down your dreams. Ask yourself the following questions:

1. Who do I want to be and what character traits do I want to possess?

_____

_____

_____

_____

2. Where do I want to go?

_____

_____

_____

_____

3. Which activities do I want to do?

_____

_____

_____

_____

4. What things do I want to have?

_____

_____

_____

_____

Create the feelings of success by pretending you are living the kind of life you have imagined until this practice affects the habits of your mind. Condition your mind to accept these thoughts and you will draw the opportunities and experiences to yourself.

Spend time daydreaming about where you want to be in life. Read about it. Study that place. Write about it in your journal. Draw it. Paint it. Let your mind run free with the possibilities of what you can attain, what you can be, and what you can accomplish. Don't be afraid of success. Let yourself be free to dream again.

DEVELOP YOUR DREAMS

It is important to recognize your desires so that you can develop those gifts and use them to nourish others. As I began to explore my interests with attention, I became devoted to my dreams. I realized that I wanted to speak and to write. But the nagging question kept haunting me, "And how would that pay the bills?"

Once I realized what I wanted, how would that be accomplished? I found that the first step was to decide to live my dream, and the "how to do it" would come later. Once the decision is made, then natural steps begin to follow. There is no other way to find and follow our calling except to take the next visible step that is before us.

The haunting question kept coming to me, "What if I'm no good?" But I discovered that competence takes work. We must embrace our passion, even when we are surrounded by imperfection. If we never allow ourselves to perform badly, we will never learn how to perform well. We must have patience with ourselves until the dull ordinary abilities turn into skill. If we wait for proficiency before we dare to do anything, our dreams will become stagnant. We need to practice with expectation and dignity. I began to realize that my skills increased as I earnestly applied myself. All I had to do was to concentrate on one thing at a time.

Share generously what you have been given, and the world's opportunities will be drawn to your love, passion, and talent. You have opportunities all around you. Talents intensify with use. Sharing your gifts strengthens and promotes them.

My dream was to speak and write, and I assure you it was an unlikely aspiration. I was not naturally skilled at speaking or writing. English was my worst subject in school. I was so shy that I would turn all red in the face and forget what I was trying to say. Yet I had a very strong desire to overcome my weaknesses and live my dream. I joined Toastmasters and for years I made a complete idiot of myself. Eventually, in 1997, I began my speaking career by conducting one simple workshop. It led to another and in 2007 I started my writing career with one newspaper article, which introduced the next one. I remember the first cheque I received for teaching a workshop. By my reaction my husband thought I had just received a huge inheritance from a lost relative. It was $75, and you couldn't have given me anything else that would have meant more to me. The feeling of coming home and being true to my calling meant more to me than any publicity, paycheck, or praise. I am proud of what I've done, but I am even more thrilled by who I've become. We will dare to become more than we ever dreamed by saying "yes" to the dreams that tug at our hearts. But it all starts with a willingness to share your abilities with the world you live in.

DETERMINE YOUR VALUES

When mapping a game plan for your life, finding meaningful work, and living your dreams, it is vital to be aware of your values. Aligning your life according to what you really value gives you the greatest success. Here is a list of values. Go through the list and pick out your top eight. Evaluate what is most important to you and always remind yourself of it, especially when you get overwhelmed with the day-to-day activities of life.

Abundance	Enjoyment	Integrity
Assertiveness	Entertainment	Intimacy
Availability	Enthusiasm	Leadership
Awareness	Excitement	Learning
Balance	Expertise	Loyalty
Beauty	Exploration	Making a difference
Belonging	Expressiveness	Organization
Boldness	Faith	Originality
Bravery	Family	Passion
Cheerfulness	Financial independence	Playfulness
Clarity	Fitness	Practicality
Clear-mindedness	Focus	Professionalism

Commitment	Freedom	Prosperity
Compassion	Friendliness	Resourcefulness
Confidence	Fun	Respect
Contribution	Generosity	Significance
Conviction	Giving	Simplicity
Cooperation	Grace	Skillfulness
Courage	Gratitude	Solitude
Creativity	Growth	Spirituality
Credibility	Guidance	Success
Decisiveness	Happiness	Support
Dependability	Health	Teamwork
Determination	Heart	Thankfulness
Direction	Helpfulness	Trustworthiness
Discipline	Honesty	Uniqueness
Discovery	Honour	Usefulness
Education	Humility	Variety
Encouragement	Humor	Vision
Endurance	Insightfulness	Wealth
Energy	Inspiration	Wisdom

HERE ARE SOME QUESTIONS TO CONSIDER

1. Describe the type of person you want to become. What do you want said about you by your family and friends?

   _____

   _____

   _____

   _____

2. What do you expect to achieve in your life?

   _____

   _____

   _____

   _____

3. What are your strengths that you can develop?

   _____

   _____

   _____

   _____

4. What do you love to do?   What makes you excited about life?

_____

_____

_____

_____

5. What type of work do you enjoy?

_____

_____

_____

_____

6. How much money would you like to earn, save, invest, or give to worthwhile cause? (We will cover this in greater detail in chapter 5)

_____

_____

_____

_____

Thinking for a Change

7. What would be your ideal fitness program? How will you take care of your body and physical appearance? (Chapter 4 deals more with this)

_____

_____

_____

_____

8. What skills would you like to acquire?

_____

_____

_____

_____

9. What would you like to do for leisure?

_____

_____

_____

_____

10. What friendships would you like to develop?

_____

_____

_____

_____

TURN YOUR GOALS INTO AFFIRMATIONS

Once you have discovered what you would like to be, have, and accomplish, you can write your goals up as affirmations. Here are some examples.

- I save for my future and I am financially independent.
- I am energetic, strong, and in good physical condition.
- I take pleasure in the caring relationships of people who love and support me.

- We are a close-knit family and we enjoy doing fun activities together and having heart-to-heart talks.

- My home is a peaceful environment that nurtures me and brings me comfort.

- My work is rewarding and I get paid for what I love to do.

- _____

RECOGNIZE THAT YOU ARE NOT YOUR OCCUPATION

One caution about fulfilling your dreams is to remember that your identity should not be based on your occupation. A couple of years ago, one of my jobs had ended for the summer and I was forced to look for employment. It felt uncomfortable asking businesses for applications and my fear of rejection tried to get the better of me. I was shocked by how much this experience affected my self-worth. I began to realize that I had allowed my identity and personal worth to be determined by what I did. I ended up getting a job cleaning the church. I felt that my personal worth went up in value when I was the speaker but when I was the custodian, I felt like less of a person.

The reality hit me that I had been guilty of placing value on others and myself according to the job description. At times it seems to give such pleasure to say things like, "I'm a teacher." As if what I do for an occupation is who I am. Am I any more of a person because I teach, or any less of a person because I clean toilets? My worth and value as an individual should be based on God's opinion about me.

Because of Christ's love for me I am important. I am valuable enough that Jesus died for me. Isn't His love and acceptance of me enough? Why do we tend to connect our identity with our occupation, as if it were the measuring stick of our worth?

Why do we treat some people as celebrities hoping they may notice us and ignore others as if they are insignificant? There are some churches where "the man of God" is untouchable. You hear a commotion and see several bodyguards as he comes up the aisle just before he preaches. As soon as he is finished preaching, he is escorted out. This sort of thing promotes separation and division from clergy and laity. Jesus is reachable to all who are hungry and thirsty for Him, regardless of their occupation.

God's opinion of us is not based on what we do for a living. The Bible says in Isaiah 1:19 that, "Those who are willing and obedient shall eat the good of the land." If my job is sweeping the street, then I should do it with dignity and excellence.

If jobs like cleaning the church are not done properly, it will have an effect on the quality of the public meetings. We all have a part to play. Maybe in the world's eyes, there is not the same personal recognition or financial reimbursement for the janitor as there is for the pastor, but the bottom line is obedience to God.

Everything we do in life is important and it is all ministry unto the Lord. As Christians we are all in full-time ministry. Everything we do is ministry. In Ecclesiastes 9:10 it says that, "Whatever your hand finds to do, do it with all your might."

So the next time your circumstances change and instead of being the "Big Cheese" you find yourself picking up the cheese off the floor, remember this: you are important in the sight of God regardless of what you do as an occupation. Don't limit your opinion of yourself by a job description. Be confident that you and others are all of equal value regardless of the type of work you do.

QUESTIONS TO THINK ABOUT

1. How can I clear my mind by clearing my environment?

_____

_____

_____

_____

_____

2. What are some areas I am over-committed in and I need to say "no" to?

_____

_____

_____

_____

_____

_____

3. What areas are priorities that I have neglected
   and I need to say "yes" to?

   _____

   _____

   _____

   _____

   _____

   _____

4. How can I conquer procrastination?

   _____

   _____

   _____

   _____

   _____

   _____

5. What things have I accomplished that I am proud of?

_____

_____

_____

_____

_____

_____

6. What are my top eight values and how can I live my life in harmony with those values?

_____

_____

_____

_____

_____

_____

_____

_____

7. What are my affirmation statements regarding my goals?

_____

_____

_____

_____

_____

8. Do I tend to connect my self-worth to my occupation? If so, how can I bring this into balance?

_____

_____

_____

_____

_____

CHAPTER 4

TRANSFORM YOUR RELATIONSHIPS TO CREATE INTIMACY

Developing relationships is important. One of the most common areas that we tend to get hurt is relationships. Sometimes when we are in pain we tend to shut everyone out so that we will not get hurt again. Yes, a lot of pain can come from relationships, but it can also provide tremendous healing.

DEAL WITH HURTS FROM THE PAST

Each of us, from time to time, must deal with disappointments that we face. We live in a world of dysfunction and sometimes we get hurt. Dealing with the hurts of our past is mandatory if we want to develop strong relationships.

It is shocking to me how much tragedy some people face. Being involved in helping youth at risk in our community has given me the wonderful opportunity of talking with a variety of teenagers and young adults. I've heard stories of betrayal, abandonment, rejection, murder, suicide, and abuse of all kinds. It's disgusting. My heart goes out to all of them and I pray that somehow they can be free from all the pain they have experienced.

We cannot ignore our hearts, minds, and souls. We must listen to what is going on inside, good or bad. We have to bring it up and deal with it. As Solomon said in Proverbs 4:23 about minding what is inside the heart: "Above all else, guard your heart, for it is the wellspring of life." It is the place from which everything comes. Success and failure alike arise from what is going on inside and the wise person is one who pays attention. With wisdom we can oversee what is going on inside and deal with it.

ACKNOWLEDGE THE PAIN

I was once faced with a situation where I felt falsely accused and unappreciated for endless hours of service and commitment. For months I had a cold that I could not get rid of and constant pain in my neck and shoulders. As I lay on my bed pondering the events that had taken place, I could not deny my pain any longer and burst into tears. The reality hit that I had been deeply wounded. As I faced my hurt and allowed myself to grieve, my tears became healing agents, cleansing my soul and dislodging the feelings of anger, hurt, pain, and sorrow. I ended by forgiving those people who had hurt me and asking Jesus to minister His love to them. I then made a decision to let go of all that pain and deal with it in constructive ways.

One of my favourite authors, Dr. Henry Cloud, in his book "Nine Things You Simply Must Do," shares nine principles to be truly effective in life. The first principle is entitled "Dig it up." He says that the reality of the life we see and live on the outside is one that emerges from the inside, from our hearts, minds, and souls. In this chapter he encourages readers to look at, listen to, discover, and be mindful of our internal life—the good things in us, like our talents, feelings, desires, and dreams as well as the bad things like our hurt, pain, anger, and negative emotions.

He goes on to say, "Get rid of the pain you carry around and the effects it is having on your life. If you ignore it, it will become a cancer that gets larger. Grief that is ignored turns into depression and hopelessness. Hurt turns into lack of trust and anger turns into bitterness and hatred. If you are walking around with unresolved matters of the heart, it is time to deal with them. When you face your demons and your pain, you 'reclaim the land' of your heart and soul. You come through that suffering better than when you went in. Process it, mourn it, heal it, grieve it, and repent of it or whatever it takes to work it out of your system." Begin to forgive those people and let go of that pain.

EXERCISE YOUR DISCERNMENT

Being honest with ourselves and with others isn't always easy. Finding a safe place to be real can be difficult at times. Knowing what to share and with whom to share it takes the gift of discernment that all of us can benefit from. There are some people who for the life of them cannot keep a secret. They don't know the meaning of "confidential." They live from one day to the next feasting upon others' weaknesses. Like vultures they are ready to devour any poor soul that dares to expose any problem areas. My advice to you is beware of such gossipers and steer clear of them. And if you have been one yourself, now is the time to change. The way you treat others will come back to you so repent and stop this hurtful behaviour.

DEAL WITH THE MONSTER

As a result of living in Abbotsford for over 32 years, I have had the privilege of knowing many people. Even people whom I don't necessarily associate with very often sometimes tell me "secrets" about their lives that are very shocking. I, too, once had a big "secret" in my life in 1999. It was like a giant monster living in my closet. I didn't know what to do with it and I lived in fear of being found out. Although both my husband, Bob, and I were in full-time Christian service, our marriage was in big trouble, heading downhill fast. When we both admitted we needed help and started receiving marriage counseling, it was refreshing to reveal our secret problems without fear of gossip.

Learning to be real and honest with ourselves and with our counselors was a true gift.

I have discovered that the more I admit my imperfections, the less frightening they become to me. When I admitted there was a monster growing in my closet, exposed it, and dealt with it, I was so liberated. As I reach out for help to those who genuinely love and care for me, I become more free to be who I am. As we discover the freedom of transparency we can encourage others with this gift too. I encourage you to expose secrets that have been weighing on you.

UNDERSTAND THE POWER OF SPOKEN WORDS

Solid relationships are built on solid communication. The words we speak to one another, our body language, and the tone of voice has a profound influence on the quality of our relationships.

I remember growing up as a child singing, "Sticks and stones may break my bones, but words will never hurt me." At the time, I thought I was being a wise person to just ignore negative words that were spoken over me. Yet years later I did not understand why I suffered with so much intimidation, fear, and rejection. I thought by sweeping those words under the carpet, so to speak, I had stopped the effect of them. I did not realize that those words had settled into my subconscious mind and were controlling me in ways I did not understand.

Perhaps being called ugly and stupid had a part to play in my insecurity. Admitting now that I was described by those words is not a sign of weakness, but rather an opportunity to change those negative beliefs into positive ones. My problems stemmed from believing those lies and accepting them as truth. Proverbs 23:7 says, "As a man thinks in his heart so is he." So now my job is to replace those lies with the truth.

As an adult, when I think back to that familiar saying of words never hurting me, I can't help but wonder who it was that came up with that absurd motto. Was it indeed a fact that words did not have an impact on the person who invented it? I think not. Maybe it wasn't until years later that he or she realized that words do influence us in positive and negative ways. To ignore negative words does not take away the effect they have on us.

CHANGING THE WAY YOU THINK CHANGES YOUR TALK

How does one control the words that come out of our mouths? Luke 6:45 tell us that out of the abundance of the heart the mouth speaks. Therefore, to change the way we talk we must first change the way we think. Philippians 4:8 tells us to think on those things that are true, noble, just, pure, lovely, and of a good report. The verse tells us that if there is any virtue and any praise in these things, we should think and meditate on them.

A person I met recently had beautiful plants in her home. When I asked her what her secret was, I was astonished at her answer. "Besides the normal watering and fertilizing," she said, "I talk to them. I tell them they are healthy and are growing strong and beautiful." She went on to tell me that she even plays pleasant music for them. I wondered that if plants could profit from kind words, how much more so could humans.

SPEAK ENCOURAGING WORDS

Proverbs 18:21 says that, "Death and life are in the power of the tongue and they who love it shall eat the fruit of it." If life and death are in the power of our tongue, why not use it for good? If we can have a positive influence in the lives of others, why not take advantage of it? Words certainly do have an impact in our lives and a few encouraging words can go a long way. There seems to be a famine in our land of uplifting words. Words like:

- "I love you."
- "You did an awesome job."
- "I'm proud of you."
- "That colour looks great on you."

Why not make a commitment today to share positive words with others?

DEAL WITH PROBLEMS QUICKLY

Relationships, like many other aspects of life, take work to make them succeed. We have a choice to either let our relationships drift backwards into neglect or put forth some effort and invest into them and see them succeed. One tendency with relationships is to take them for granted and not deal with the problems staring us in the face.

I had encountered a situation that caused me to wonder why we tend to wait until the last minute before getting things resolved. Why do we let things slide into neglect instead of attending to problems before they get out of hand?

My daughter wanted a cell phone and thought it might be a good idea for me to have one too. We signed up for a plan but for some reason the phone that I received was a "lemon." After hours of programming it and putting all my phone numbers and music into it, the battery crashed and the phone was dead. I could not even charge it. I went back to the store in my frustration and asked for a different type of phone. They said I could not receive a different type because I had thrown the box away. They gave me a new phone, but it was the same kind. Again, only after a few days, the new phone crashed again. Now I was really getting annoyed. I went back to the store and again asked for a different kind of phone. They repeated to me, that I could not have a different phone and gave me the same type of phone. The third phone crashed again and died on me.

I phoned customer service and they admitted that I had been unrightfully treated. They were willing to give me a different type of phone. But it was too late for me. I was past the point of wanting a new phone; by this time, all I wanted was to cancel the account. If two weeks earlier they would have offered me a different type of phone, I would have gladly received it. Now, I was too frustrated and ended up sending the phone back and cancelling my account.

It reminded me of a friend of mine who for several months kept asking her husband to go to marriage counseling with her. After being denied several times, and with problems escalating, one day she came to him and said she wanted a divorce. He suddenly agreed to marriage counseling, but she said, "Honey, it's too late for that. I asked you several times to come with me to marriage counseling and you refused. Now I want out of the commitment." In other words she wanted to "cancel the account." I felt sad for my friends that they were not able to resolve it. They may have succeeded if only they had paid attention to the problem before it got to the point where she was now too discouraged to resolve it.

DEVELOP YOUR RELATIONSHIP WITH GOD

This also involves our relationship with God. I have heard many stories of people waiting until their death bed before making things right with God. Suddenly they have to face the reality of death and where that may lead them. Isn't having a relationship with God more important that just being saved from hell? If my spiritual condition needs attention, now is the time to cry out to God. Why wait until my last breath?

It is a lesson for all of us. Don't wait for problems to get out of control. Deal with them right away. Do what it takes to rectify the situation as quickly as possible. James 4:10 says, "Humble yourself in the sight of God, repent and confess your sins and He will lift you up." What problem has been staring you in the face that needs your special attention?

For me, believing that there is someone up there looking out for my best interest gives me the courage to continue on. My belief in God, talking to Him, and reading the Bible is my source of strength and power. When I encounter problems and call out in the Name of Jesus, I know He hears me and He answers me. He is the source of my hope and faith.

If I only had myself to depend on, I would be in a sorry state. But to know someone bigger than myself has the last say gives me strength to continue on.

ENHANCE YOUR RELATIONSHIP WITH YOUR SPOUSE

Building a solid relationship with your significant other takes effort. Let's not fool ourselves by thinking we can just cruise through our marriage without working at it. I have noticed that any time I drift through life I am sliding backwards, not moving ahead. It is no different in a marriage relationship. It is too easy to drift through married life only to suddenly discover you are headed for divorce.

I remember when dating was so much fun, but what happened after we got married? That's when the mundane day-to-day routine began to dampen our relationship. We realized that we needed to stir up the romance and put the spark back in our relationship.

Here are some ways you too can add zip and pizzazz to your marriage.

1. Schedule weekly dates with your partner. Set aside one night a week and take turns planning the date. Why stop dating just because you are married?

2. Develop open communication by sharing ideas, thoughts, concerns, joys, and sorrows with each other. Go for a half-hour walk together each day.

3. Be romantic with each other. Give flowers, special meals, gifts, love notes, hugs, acts of kindness, or words of encouragement. Find out what turns your loved one on.

4. If your sex life has gone stale, read books or listen to CDs on the subject. (I recommend Ed

Wheat's material found at Christian Book Stores.)

5. Accept your partner fully. Stop trying to change him or her and focus on changing yourself. Take notice of all the good qualities and freely hand out sincere compliments.

6. Plan a second honeymoon. Once in a while plan a weekend away at a hotel for just the two of you. Go out for dinner, do something that's fun, watch a love show, go for a swim, eat chocolate, or have a fondue.

7. Make time for yourself. If you feel tired and stressed, rejuvenate yourself by taking care of your own needs. Don't expect your partner to meet all your needs.

8. Decorate your bedroom for romance. Put a lock on the door, play soft relaxing music, light candles, use soft sheets, massaging oils, soothing smells, favourite colours, flowers, or whatever brings you pleasure.

9. Simplify your lifestyle. Slow down. Most couples are too tired for each other. They are working so hard just to get the bills paid that they seldom have a chance to enjoy each other. Ask yourself where you can cut back and start saying "no" to time wasters.

Your partner will be delighted as you take an active part in applying some of these tips. Remember to celebrate every day together. Your sweetheart will keep coming back for more.

BE ON THE SAME TEAM

Building strong relationships is about being on the same team. Although not always an easy task, working together in unity has many wonderful benefits. Ecclesiastes 4:9–12 says, "Two are better than one, because they have a good reward for their labour. If they fall, one will lift up his companion, but woe to him who is alone when he falls, for he has no one to help him up. Again, if two lie down together, they will keep warm, but how can one be warm alone? Though one may be overpowered by another, two can withstand him. And a threefold cord is not quickly broken." Whether you are a parent, the head of an organization, or any other kind of leader, learning to develop a team is foundational for developing healthy relationships. If you want to get something done, having an effective team working together is vital.

When our children were two and four years old, they always wanted to help with washing the dishes. At times I felt so frustrated I could hardly contain myself. Their shirts were soaked in water and a big puddle had formed on the floor under the two chairs they stood on. The dishes had so much soap on them that I had to rinse the dishes all over again. I so badly wanted them to just go and play so that I would do the work myself. I shared my frustration with a good friend (much wiser than myself). She told me to continue with letting them help me. She said they would get into the habit of helping me and one day I would appreciate it. She was right. To this day our children still wash dishes for me and I do appreciate it immensely.

Building a team takes skill and requires strategic planning. Here are six steps in building a winning team.

1. Develop the ability to communicate the vision. Determine what the purpose of the team is. What are you trying to achieve?
2. Respond to the needs of your team members. There are five basic needs people have when they are working as a team.
   - Autonomy. Give them freedom to contribute and incorporate their own ideas.

- Equality of opportunity. Don't show favouritism. Treat them all as equals.
- Meaningful work. There must be a sense of accomplishment.
- A share in the profits. What's in it for them?
- A sense of belonging. They must know they are a vital part of the team and are associated with you.

3. Cultivate a willingness to delegate authority. Let them know that you believe they can do their jobs without constant supervision.

4. Nurture a tolerance for experimentation and failure. Encourage them to be open to experiment, let them take chances, and don't punish them for it. You have to be calm about mistakes.

5. Understand that your teammates must compensate for your weaknesses. You need each other.

6. Acquire an ability to motivate each member of the team. Find out what stimulates and encourages them.

RECOGNIZE THE POWER OF INFLUENCE

Working together with a common goal can be an exhilarating experience. We have a surprisingly profound influence on each other and we must use it for the good. I grew up believing that we are islands unto ourselves, affecting nobody in the decisions we make. I believed that we could choose not to allow the behaviour of others to affect us. Somehow, unconsciously, I believed that I would be safe from negative experiences by accepting this philosophy. It was not until I accepted the fact that we are influenced by each other that I began to realize the benefits of proper interaction.

For most of my life, I believed men were superior to women, and the role of women is to make men look good. This belief gave me an excuse to remain insecure, fearful, and passive. However, during the last ten years of our marriage, my husband Bob has changed my belief, thus transforming me into a new person. His positive influence towards me has affected me in ways I do not understand. Insecure, passive, and fearful no longer describe who I am, thanks to him.

In 1983 when I married Bob, who was a youth pastor at the time, I believed that my role as his wife was to hide in his shadow. Yet as the years unfolded, I could not deny my unhappiness. I went into a deep depression, confused about my identity, and I lost my dream of any public ministry. Many of the local pastors did not know my first name, but would refer to me as "Bob's wife."

When Bob and I started receiving marriage counseling, my belief that I was an island unto myself was a major threat to our relationship. Learning to work beside Bob as a team instead of being in competition was a major factor in us restoring our relationship. The counselor challenged my belief that women's position in life is to serve men. He summed it up this way, "Right now, Alice, you have responsibility without authority, and Bob, you have authority without responsibility. This must change."

Ephesians 5:22 says, "Wives submit to your own husbands, as to the Lord, for the husband is the head of the wife." The word head means protector and guard. The wife and children are a reflection of the care of the husband. As a gardener tends his garden, so too does the husband take care of his wife and children. It goes on to say that husbands must love their wives and each should submit to the other. The years that followed were an opportunity to learn how to balance the scale regarding this issue of equality. My sense of well-being was directly related to the way in which I was treated as a woman.

Women in this city and across this nation desire to contribute to society, but we can only do so when we are given freedom and liberty. We do influence one another and men have an incredible opportunity to allow women to come out of their shadows and contribute to society in more visible ways. Even within the church, putting people in the right positions, regardless of gender, contributes to the well-being of the team as a whole. As authority is delegated to members based on giftedness, character, and calling, regardless of gender, everyone benefits from it. God is raising up women to stand alongside one another and, as men make room for us, everyone will profit from the positive influence that we have.

USE FEEDBACK TO OVERCOME BLIND SPOTS

One amazing benefit of relationships is that it can offer feedback to help us overcome our blind spots. One of the joys of being a parent is raising teenagers. I remember when our children were teenagers and I had the honour of teaching them how to drive a car.

One of the lessons in driving is to understand and discover what a blind spot is. When our teenagers were learning to drive, one of them would need to get into the left lane, only to discover that suddenly a vehicle appeared out of nowhere. As the horrified instructor I wondered how my young driver could not have seen the vehicle. What was so plain and easy for me to see could not be seen by the driver because it was in a "blind spot." To overcome blind spots while driving, shoulder checks come into play. But how do we conquer blind spots in our personal lives?

At university in one of my courses I learned a concept called the "Jeharvi Window." It is a definition of who we are. The window is divided up into four parts or four squares. One part of who we are consists of our public self. This consists of things known to us and known to others. A second part of us is our private self which consists of things that are known to us but is not known to others. There is another part of us that is known to others but is not known to us. This area is called our blind spots. Lastly there is a part of us that is not known to us or to others; only God knows. To conquer this area we must be dependant on God to reveal these things to us.

While mentoring young adults in this community, I am amazed at how good the majority of them are at seeing the faults of their fellow group members. Yet when it comes to admitting their own areas of weakness, they are very ineffective.

Jesus addressed these blind spots by telling us to take the log out of our own eye first so we may see clearly to take the speck out of our brother's eye (Matthew 7:3).

Barbara Wentroble, in her book *Freedom from Deception*, says that one of the reasons people get deceived is because they have an independent spirit. She says, "Every person needs someone to help him see his blind spots. None of us see everything clearly. We were created to need each other. Sometimes reports are heard about ministers who fall into immorality or greed. Later, we discover that they were not accountable to any other leader. They were led away from the truth by their own human nature without anyone to keep them accountable. Being accountable to a spiritually mature group will prevent the enemy from blinding our eyes to deception."

We may not totally eliminate our blind spots but we can reduce them significantly by receiving feedback from others. Allowing others to point out our blind spots is not for the faint-hearted. It takes maturity to ask for and receive feedback, but it is a tool designed to help you overcome your weaknesses. This is not a time to argue or become defensive, but rather a time to listen. Take some time afterwards to ponder what was said and make a plan to implement a strategy for change.

QUESTIONS TO THINK ABOUT

1. Is there anyone who has hurt me that I need to forgive?

   _____

   _____

   _____

   _____

2. Is there a relationship that I need to let go of because it is toxic and harmful to me?

   _____

   _____

   _____

   _____

3. What types of words come out of my mouth? Do my words build others up or tear others down?

_____

_____

_____

_____

_____

_____

4. Who am I thankful for in my life and how can I express my appreciation to them?

_____

_____

_____

_____

_____

_____

5. Who are the people that are important to me? How can I show love for them in practical ways?

_____

_____

_____

_____

_____

_____

6. How can I work together with others more as a team?

_____

_____

_____

_____

_____

_____

7. Do I believe men and women are equal? How do my actions demonstrate this belief?

     _____

     _____

     _____

     _____

     _____

8. What feedback have I received that has been helpful to me?

     _____

     _____

     _____

     _____

     _____

9. What areas of my life do I need to be accountable in?

_____

_____

_____

_____

_____

_____

Thinking for a Change

CHAPTER 5
TRANSFORM YOUR ECONOMICAL SITUATION TO GAIN FINANCIAL FREEDOM

Getting your finances in order, just like any other area of your life, takes discipline and self-control. As a child, I was not taught how to manage money. I had no concept of how to get it, manage it, or invest it. As soon as I had a little money in my hands, my mind went to work calculating all the things I wanted and I had no peace until all the money was spent.

Even as an adult, I gave all my cheques to my husband and I just let him take care of our financial well-being. But over the years, I grew bitter in having no money and the debt grew bigger, my spending increased, and it became more out of control, all while the insecurity amplified.

One day I remember getting to the place where I had enough. Tears of regret oozed out of

103

me like puss from a sore. I hung my head in sorrow and cried myself to sleep. The next morning, I made a fresh commitment to start a new financial path. At that point I decided that my days of living from paycheck to paycheck were over. No more allowing my wants to get out of control. No more blaming others for my financial problems. It was time for me to replace self-indulgence with self-control. It was time to confront my financial problems and learn important lessons.

I had to forgive others for taking advantage of me and I had to forgive myself for being naive and lazy concerning finances. Instead of messing around with symptoms, I had to deal with the root causes of my dysfunction. I began to diagnose my beliefs about finances and I discovered that my beliefs were just plain wrong. Here are my erroneous convictions:

- It is impossible to solve my financial problems.

- Trying to resolve my financial problems and plan for my future is wrong, because only God knows the future.
- The world will come to an end soon, so there's no point in planning because I have no control over my future.

Those beliefs caused me to become financially careless.

IDENTIFY WHAT YOU BELIEVE ABOUT MONEY

What do you believe about money? What kind of relationship do you have with money? I am now sure that money has power. It is alive. If you don't control it and tell it what to do, it will rule you and become your master.

Are you the slave of money? Do you ask it, "money, may I do this, or go there?" Do you base your decisions on whether or not money is available? You must tell your money what to do, or it will control you.

Many people think that money makes them happy. I can tell you that money does not make you happy. Money only makes you more of what you already are. If a person enjoys drinking alcohol and suddenly gets a lot of money, guess what he or she ends up spending money on? The possibility of more money only increases their chances of becoming an alcoholic. The same is true with entertainment, food, shopping, giving, or saving—whatever you do with your money, it is a reflection of what type of person you are and having more money only increases that.

Here is a list of beliefs about money. Read the following statements and see which ones you believe to be true.

- This country is going down the tubes, so I'll spend as much as I can now and I won't plan for my future because if I don't spend all my money now someone else will later.

- I often dream about all the things I would do if I had more money.

- Spending money is my reward for all my work.

- I will get what I want now and pay later.

- If I get more money, it will ruin me and destroy my morals. I will become a bad person.

- I don't have the necessary skill to make more money or to handle it.

- I know in my head I should save money, but I can't and I don't want to.

- My worth is based upon how much money I have.

- The more I have, the more I want; I am never satisfied with enough.

- Managing money is too hard and takes up too much time.

- If I don't handle money correctly, other people will bail me out.
- It is a waste of time planning financial strategies when I could be doing spiritual activities.
- I don't want more money because then I have to be responsible for it.
- People who save money never have any fun.
- If people are wealthy it means that they love money.
- If I give to others that means there will be less for me.
- God's love for people is based on how much money they have.
- If I have more money people will respect me more.
- Wealthy people use illegal means to get their money.
- _____
- _____

FIND WORK YOU LOVE TO DO

Work is a very large part of our lives and it's important to know how to make the most of it. Do you work just to pay the bills or do you work to contribute to life? Mark Fisher, in his book *The Instant Millionaire*, says that to be a millionaire you must love your work and enjoy your occupation.

I began to notice what I was good at and what gave me pleasure. Again, it was not an overnight journey for me, but eventually I became a Life Coach in 1997 and to this day, I still love my work. It was not easy in the beginning. It took a lot of commitment and it included taking a lot of risks. But I went back to school and received the education I needed to upgrade my skills. I read books to gain confidence and I reached out to others for help. It took a lot of dedication and hard work, but now I enjoy the benefits and the income from doing what I love to do. And the best part of all the sacrifices I had made at that time is that now I am reaping all the benefits and enjoying the rewards. The joy of helping others to make positive changes in their lives makes all my struggles worth it.

Sixty percent of our lives (or more) is spent on working, so why not enjoy it? In retail stores I sometimes meet cashiers and sales clerks who hate their jobs. I think it is so unfortunate to be miserable every day like that. If you dislike your job maybe it's time you start taking some concrete steps towards changing it.

Here are some ways to explore and transition yourself into finding work you love.

- Investigate new things and discover what you enjoy and what you are good at. Ask other people and take assessments and personality tests.

- Find a job that allows you to do the activities that you enjoy doing.
- If your day job pays the bills, then use your evenings to develop your passion.
- Work part time and live your passion part time. Eventually you can quit your day job and follow your dream full time.
- If your job is too demanding and stressful, you may need to climb down the ladder to the right job.
- Take a sabbatical. If you are able to, take some time off and focus on living your dream.
- Find a job that lets you leave and come back again.

READ GOOD BOOKS

Read between 1 and 4 books each month. Gain wisdom and implement it into your own life.

Trying new concepts out is like putting on a new sweater. See how it fits and make the necessary adjustments. You must test and try new methods to see what is beneficial and effective in your own life.

I have read over 350 books. I underline my books, write in them, and read some of them several times. I write a list of how I will implement the things they suggest and I apply it to my own life. It's all part of changing my beliefs and the way I think about things.

Every time you read a book, it is like you have that author personally mentoring you and speaking into your life. It is the most inexpensive way I know of to receive helpful information. There is also a lot of free information on the Internet that is easy to access and very useful to apply. There is no excuse for ignorance. The Bible says in Hosea 4:6 that people are destroyed from a lack of knowledge. Ignorance is no longer an excuse. If you don't know how to manage your financial situation there is help available for you. It involves making a commitment to learn and a dedication to implement the financial principles. Just knowing something is useless but doing what you know to do will cause growth and change.

Proverbs 9:9 says "Give instruction to a wise man, and he will be still wiser. Teach a just man, and he will increase in learning."

FOLLOW GUIDELINES IN HANDLING YOUR MONEY

Living in a world that is addicted to shopping and entertainment can make saving money and staying out of debt a challenge. I fell into the trap of living beyond my means. My husband Bob and I were at one time over $52,000 in debt and had absolutely no assets. Even by paying more than our minimal payments on all our credit cards, we could not see a way out. It was not an overnight process, but slowly, one step at a time, with God's help, we began to dig ourselves out of the horrible pit of debt.

It requires a conscious effort to go against the tide. All the commercials, magazine ads, and media made me feel dissatisfied with what I had and convinced me that something new would make me feel better. Yet the more I bought, the more I wanted and the more I felt dissatisfied. I was trying to fill an emotional need. I was so addicted to shopping that I had to stop going to the shopping malls. I started buying books that kept me at home instead of wandering in the stores. I became accountable. Bob and I wrote up a budget and stuck to it.

Proverbs 25:28 tells us, "Whoever has no rule over his own spirit and has no self-control, is like a city broken down, without walls." Being out of control and careless with our finances caused a lot of frustration.

Some people think that getting out of debt just requires making more money. Although learning how to increase your income is part of the solution, it also requires managing the money you presently do have.

Here are some simple guidelines in getting your finances in order. I recommend that you engage a professional who can keep you accountable and help you develop a game plan.

1. Give 10 percent of your income to worthy causes and to your church if you attend one. As you give and help others, the law of sowing and reaping comes into effect and new money will start coming your way. Proverbs 3:9 tells us to "Honour the Lord with your possessions, and with the first fruits of all your increase."

2. Save an emergency fund of three to six months' worth of expenses. It is a wise decision to have money set aside for a rainy

day. Unforeseen things happen, like the transmission needing to be replaced in your car, the fridge quitting, the hot water tank needing replacement, or your job suddenly coming to an end. Proverbs 21:20 says, "There is desirable treasure and oil in the dwelling of the wise, but a foolish man squanders it."

3. Design a budget and live by it. If you are married make sure both of you have input and that you agree on it. It usually takes two to three months to create a budget that works. It comes by trial and error. Eventually you will discover how much money it takes for each category to live on. We would put our money in envelopes and when the $500 for grocery money was gone, it was peanut butter sandwiches the rest of the month.

4. Pay off all debt. As soon as a credit card goes one month without you paying it off, quit using it. Keep all your bills current and any extra

money you have should be put towards your debts. Call your creditors and let them know you are in the process of paying them off. I remember calling my dentist and letting him know that I would try my best to pay off the $1,500 bill as soon as I could. An hour later, he called me back and cancelled the loan. This may be rare, but people do appreciate a call to let them know what's going on. According to Proverbs 22:7, when you owe money, you are the servant to the lender.

5. Save for your future. Save for your retirement and pay your house off. Sixty-five percent of the population of Canada has no pension plan.

6. Save up for purchases and pay cash for them. Do not purchase anything on credit. A friend of mine opened a bank account for her two daughters when they were born. Every month she put into their bank account the child tax

credit. By the age of 19, they both had money saved up for a car.

7. Use a Visa debit card for online purchases or check with your bank for an alternative. Regular credit cards can get out of hand and for people who can not pay it off each month, it is better to not have regular credit cards.

8. Invest part of your income in order to create other streams of income. There are many ways to invest your money and many books that specialize in this subject. It could include stocks and bonds, mutual funds, RRSPs, owning your own business, and buying real estate, just to mention a few.

CLEARLY DEFINE YOUR FINANCIAL GOALS

When a person is overwhelmed by a problem, the natural tendency is to fall into self-pity and hopelessness. It seems so easy at the time, just to give up, collect excuses, and play the "blame game." A strategy that proves to be effective for me is to have a new vision. Instead of being consumed by my painful circumstances, I begin to create a new image in my mind of what I want. Although it seems impossible at the time, I start visualizing my new goals. I think about them. I meditate on them. I write them down and have pictures that remind me of what I want.

With your finances, as in any area, you must be convinced that you will succeed. Bring your thoughts and actions into harmony. Write a list of your financial goals within the next five years. Aim high but don't curse yourself if you don't reach them all. Here is an example.

- A house worth $500,000
- A second home in the country worth $300,000
- No more personal debts
- $300,000 in cash and other liquid assets

- $300,000 invested
- $500,000 invested in property, which grows to $3,000,000 in equity within five years from the time of purchase
- A successful business that allows me to travel internationally
- A cook and a housekeeper

ESTABLISH NEW BELIEFS ABOUT YOUR FINANCES

If you don't like where you are at in life, start asking yourself what you believe to be true about your situation. Once you identify what you believe, you can then begin to change it. Here are examples of new beliefs concerning finances. Adapt them as your own or make up new ones. The key is to speak affirmations over yourself everyday to replace your negative beliefs concerning finances.

- Every day, in every way, I am getting better and better.
- Every day I do what I love to do. I follow my passion, I am good at it and the money follows.
- I am making a living doing every day what I love to do. My money is my servant.
- By the end of this year I will possess assets (investments, savings, real estate, mutual funds) worth $310,250. I will double those assets for five years.
- I am happily earning, saving, and investing $10,000 a month ($120,000 a year).
- I work with people I love in a wonderful location.
- I live a life of discipline and I do what is necessary to implement what I learn.
- God takes my little efforts and rewards them with great success.

- God brings all the right people across my path to enhance my life and ministry. They support and encourage me in pursuing my dreams.
- Multiple streams of income and positive cash flow are opening up for me.

Today is the first day of the rest of your life. It is never too late to make new changes in your life if you start now. Develop a support system around you and start telling yourself that with God's help you too can start thinking for a change.

QUESTIONS TO THINK ABOUT

1. What do you believe about money? Are these beliefs negative or positive?

    _____

    _____

    _____

    _____

2. What type of work do you love to do?

    _____

    _____

    _____

    _____

3. What new habits will you introduce into your
    life to turn your finances around?

    _____

    _____

    _____

    _____

For your free 35 Simple Secrets Towards A Life
Makeover (value $19), visit our website at
www.dynamicchanges.ca.

Thinking for a Change

RECOMMENDED READING

Self-esteem

Believing in Yourself _by Earnie Larsen and Carol Hegarty_

This small devotional book is divided up into daily sections to make it an easy read. This is an excellent book for those who struggle with addictions. The authors cover eleven main topics related to self-esteem. These topics include: acceptance, accomplishments, anger, attitude, dealing with the past, forgiveness, habits, relationships, risk-taking, self-care, and self-talk.

The Search for Significance _by Robert S. McGee_

This book helped me to change the way I felt about myself. Mr. McGee reveals traps that can easily ensnare us when it comes to the way we feel about ourselves. He covers topics such as performance, approval, blame, shame, and guilt.

His deep belief in God allows the reader to draw love from God. God loves you and you can receive His love even if you feel there is no human love to be found. This love in return will help you to love and accept yourself.

Discover Who You Are *by Jane A.G. Kise, David Stark and Sandra Krebs Hirsh*

This book will help you to discover yourself. It helps you to understand your interests, priorities, values, gifts, personality, and passions. This book will give you practical ways to accept who you are and shine in your areas of giftedness.

Health

The Seven Pillars of Health *by Don Colbert, MD*

This is a simple-to-understand and easy-to-read guideline on how to manage your health. There is also a workbook that can be used with it. It is full of helpful ideas to bring balance to your life.

The seven main areas (or pillars) are water, sleep, food, exercise, detoxification, nutritional supplements, and coping with stress. It is loaded with benefits and reasons why we should take care of our health.

<u>Accomplishments</u>

Getting Things Done by David Allen

This book is filled with practical steps on how you can increase your capacity to get more things done. Mr. Allen shares a system that you can use to organize, schedule, and plan every aspect of your life. After reading his book and implementing his strategies I was impressed with how much more I could complete by being more organized and focused.

This Time I Dance by Tama J. Kieves

This is a delightful book that motivated and inspired me to take new risks in my life. Ms. Kieves' story is amazing and she speaks from the heart. The insights she shares are sure to give you new strength to take responsibility for your life. She is an inspiration to me and I know will be to you too.

Take Back Your Life by Odette Pollar

This is a practical book to help you learn how to live a simpler life. She helps to bring clarity to whatever means the most in your life and shows how to get rid of anything else that clutters your mind and space. It is full of tips to get your life back on track by managing your time, managing your thoughts, and managing your priorities.

Coach Yourself to Success by Talane Miedaner

This is a delightful and easy read. It is full of practical ways you can enhance your life in many different areas. It helped to give me the motivation and determination to do whatever it takes to bring my life into balance. It is full of insightful information to get you thinking.

Relationships

Raising Positive Kids in a Negative World by Zig Ziglar

I read this book in 1990 when our children were very young. I have used the concepts in this book for parenting and it has been extremely helpful. Mr. Ziglar encourages readers to invest into the lives of their children. Parenting is one of the most difficult and most rewarding jobs I have ever done and this book gave me practical tips on how to be a better parent.

Boundaries by Dr. Henry Cloud and Dr. John Townsend

This book is a 'must read' for people who are unhappy in their relationships. Most unhealthy relationships are rooted in boundary issues. This book has transformed my life and I highly recommend it to make positive changes in your life. After reading it you will learn how to say "no" to the bad and say "yes" to the good.

Economics

Making a Living Without a Job by Barbara J. Winter

This has been one of my favourite books in discovering what I want to be when I grow up. It has very practical steps in how you can live your dreams. It contains self-discovery tips which are essential for living an authentic life. When I read it, it gave me the courage to step out of my comfort zone and start my own business.

Duct Tape Marketing by John Jantsch

When it comes to managing your own business, this is one of the best books I can recommend. It is full of practical steps on how to set up and market your own business. I have read this book several times because it is heavily loaded with practical things to implement into your own business.

101 Reasons Why You Must Write A Book by Bob Burnham and Jeff McCallum

If you love to write and are passionate about a certain topic, this book is for you. It is full of practical ways you can write a book, publish it, and market your book. It will motivate you to write a book and it is full of ideas in how to promote your book. Mr. Burnham was very instrumental in getting my book published.

The One Minute Millionaire by Robert Allen and Mark Victor Hansen

This book will help to give you a millionaire mindset. It gives practical steps in handling your money and it will challenge you in what you believe about money. The author states that you are your greatest asset or liability. He gives you ideas in how to tap into your genius. He also gives practical tips for marketing your own business.

The Total Money Makeover by David Ramsey

This book offers practical help in getting your finances in order. He covers topics such as dealing with debt, saving for emergencies, retirement investing, college funds, paying off your mortgage, and building wealth. Mr. Ramsey also offers a thirteen-week course through DVDs that may be available in your city. It's called *Dave Ramsey's Financial Peace University*; you can check it out on the Web.

LaVergne, TN USA
20 January 2010
170674LV00004B/4/P